The Partner's Purpose During Pregnancy

Matthew Morris

ISBN 979-8-9902789-0-5 (paperback)

ISBN 979-8-9902789-1-2 (hardcover)

ISBN 979-8-9902789-2-9 (ebook)

Library of Congress Control Number 2024905960

www.thepartnerspu.com

First Edition

DADICATION

To my wife, Shanon.

You make me brave.

CONTENTS

FOREWARD

BY: SHANON MORRIS

I hopped on and we took off!

Since I can remember, I was adamant that I would never get married or have kids. I hated dolls, I ran away when my cousins asked me to hold their babies, and I specifically stated in my 4th-grade journal that I would never be a mom.

One can only imagine my surprise when I changed my mind at the ripe age of 30, all because of a crazy cowboy named Matthew.

In fact, I was so burnt out from dating when I met him, that our first date was supposed to be my last first date before taking a hiatus from dating and pouring all of my energy into my career. Little did I know that it would quite literally be my last first date... ever. 2 weeks after we met, Matthew sat me down and told me he wanted to date me exclusively. I thought he was joking, but went along with it to see if he would keep his word.

He did.

A few months later, he accompanied me to a work conference in Las Vegas while he was recovering from foot surgery. On the last day, he won a pistol at a shooting competition (while wearing a unicorn onesie... because why not). When the event host handed him the pistol he won, he clumsily got down on his good knee and proposed. Seeing as I didn't think my life could get any more absurd, I told him I'd marry him if he got an engagement tattoo (his first) that night in lieu of rings.

What happened in Vegas didn't stay in Vegas.

The morning of our wedding, I told him he didn't have to go through with it, and that I'd understand if he wasn't ready yet. Rather than bailing, he told me to put on my swimsuit, grabbed my hand, and screamed "HOP ON AND HOLD ON" as we jumped off the dock into Lake Granbury in the middle of December.

A couple of days later, he blurted out the words "I'm ready to be a Dad with you."

This time, I believed him.

Although starting a family was not in my original life plan, I opened up to the idea because Matthew demonstrated his commitment to me, our relationship, and our family over and over again. From the day I removed my IUD to the day our daughter was born 13 months later, we've survived layoffs, military transitions, a 10,000-mile road trip, 3 months in Europe, navigating medical systems in multiple countries, moving to Chicago, and giving birth to our firstborn in our living room. I give him a lot of credit for my ability to have the birth I wanted, the health and wellness of our newborn baby girl, and my relatively uneventful postpartum recovery because he was by my side EVERY step of the way.

When I was hangry, huge, and tired, he cooked me well-balanced meals, accompanied me to the gym, and encouraged me to nap often.

When I was frantically Googling the accuracy of fundal lengths, he was on the phone with our doula, the midwives, and his primary care provider, figuring out how "urgent" our situation was and how to schedule a last-minute fetal growth ultrasound.

When I went completely "internal" during active labor (as we knew I would), he managed everything "external," from calling the midwives to translating my grunts for the birth team when I needed to push from a different position (e.g. against the dance pole in our living room).

From what I've seen on the "mommy forums," our international research, and talking to friends, family, and mentors, this isn't normal.

But, it *should* be.

And, it *can* be.

It's not rocket science... or quantum physics... or trying to decipher what women want. It's simply a matter of being there, being present, and being involved.

Watching Matthew take our 10-week-old daughter into the bathroom, and listening to his conversation with her about potty training as he's taking care of business so I can have the brain space to finish editing this book reaffirms my decision to hop on and hold on to the roller coaster that is our life together. Matthew's involvement during my pregnancy not only helped me navigate the chaos, but also gave him perspective, understanding, and most of all, **purpose**.

S.L.M.

AUTHOR'S NOTE

When I found out that my wife Shanon was pregnant, my immediate question was "How can I help?" I read pregnancy manuals, new dad guides, and even religious novels. They all have a place in my library now, but *nothing I read answered my question*. The guidebook I was looking for simply didn't exist. After listening to me gripe about it for months, Shanon finally told me "If it's not out there, get off your ass and write it." So here we are.

The purpose of this book is to answer the question:

"How can I help?"

These are NOT theoretical or hypothetical ideas conjured up in a think tank, nor is this medical information of any kind. These ARE concrete examples of how to support your partner during the 10-month wait BEFORE you enter into parenthood.

I wish someone had handed this to me when we walked out of our first ultrasound. Instead, all I got was a pat on the back and the reassuring "You'll figure it out." This book exists so you don't have to "figure it out."

What I did to support my wife applies to ANYONE wishing to be supportive during their partner's pregnancy.

Since I wrote this from my experience supporting Shanon during her pregnancy, I refer to the birthing person as "YBM" (your baby's mother) and use her pronouns.

Before my obsession with poppyseeds throws anyone off, I need to clarify that we refer to our daughter as "Baby Poppyseed" or "Poppyseed." Shanon and I were fortunate to have found out about her pregnancy when our daughter was about the size of a poppy seed, so the name stuck. No matter how old she gets or how much she grows, our daughter will always be our Poppyseed. Not to mention, I've already composed my first hit single "Poppyseed Be Poppin'," so changing her nickname now would be too confusing.

Finally, this is a living document and I want your feedback. When you find a technique or practice that strengthens your purpose as the husband, dad, boyfriend, wife, mother, co-parent, supportive friend, or a title that I have not even been exposed to yet, please share it with me via our website (www.thepartnerspurpose.com) so we can continue to hone in on the partner's purpose.

M.J.M.

THE PARTNER'S PURPOSE IS TO...

BE THERE

Ironically enough, on Mother's Day 2023, minutes after we set our bags down after a wild weekend celebrating our friend's wedding, I heard a shriek from upstairs that changed my life. I sprinted into the house, thinking the worst, only to find Shanon on the staircase waving around a handful of pregnancy tests. Once I realized that she was trying to tell me that she was pregnant, my heart exploded—not physically, as I have the heart of a Texas Mustang—but, every emotion from joy and excitement to fear and terror, hit me in the amount of time it took to get to the top of the stairs and squeeze her. When I saw the 2 pink lines for myself, the next gut punch I felt was: if I was having all these "feelz," what in the world was Shanon feeling?

After that, I knew that my priority was to be there through the good news like gender reveals and first heartbeats, to the chaos of ER visits and dealing with "medical professionals." Mistakes and hard knocks aside, my purpose was to be by Shanon's side.

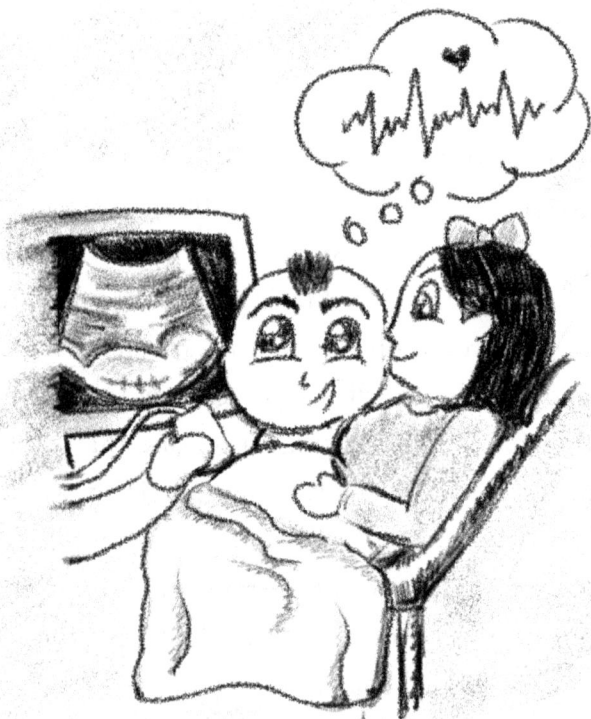

<u>Your Purpose</u>

Prioritize being present:

- Physically

- Mentally

- Emotionally

Make time to be there for, and with, your baby's mother (YBM[1]).

Partner Pro-tip: *If you're truly in a situation that prevents you from physically being present during the pregnancy, set a **minimum** of 15 minutes aside every week to check in with your partner, whether that's in person, over the phone, or via video chat.*

Email/text only as a last resort.

Partner Pro-tip +1: *If your job requires you to be away and unable to communicate for long periods of time (looking at you active duty folks), help her establish a support system **before** you leave. This is the time to call on family, friends, neighbors, and/or the local spouse's club to make sure YBM has a reliable local network to lean on that you **both** trust.*

---

1. See author's note

LOVE YOUR PARTNER FIRST

As Shanon's pregnancy progressed, I felt myself focusing less on her and more on our daughter. For a while, our conversations always seemed to gravitate toward what Poppyseed[1] needed first.

Once we recognized the strain this put on our relationship, we set out to find a new "us" activity focused on Shanon's well-being. Since Shanon's "happy place" is the gym, we decided to take bi-weekly exercise classes together until 3 days before she went into labor. This allowed us to deliberately set time aside for her mental (and physical) health while giving us something else to look forward to other than Baby Poppyseed's arrival.

---

1. See author's note

<u>Your Purpose</u>

Embrace the fact that you will put your baby first. It's natural to want to ensure their entry into the world is safe, speedy, and supported. When you feel yourself prioritizing your baby over your partner, pause and do something just for YBM:

- Get cleaned up and take her on a proper date. Remember, the best accessory in your wardrobe is who you have on your arm (remind her she is your #1).

- Cook something she loves. Learn what she enjoys, how to make it, and then serve it with a smile.

- Give her alone time. Her world is about to revolve around your baby, so give her some time to herself.

If you know what makes her feel like she is on a pedestal, do it. If you don't, this is the perfect opportunity to learn.

STAY HEALTHY TOGETHER

Did you know that maintaining a regular physical fitness regime, ceasing your intake of alcohol & processed foods, and abstaining from tobacco, and drugs (recreational and pharmaceutical) increases your chances of producing healthy sperm? Did you also know that following these same practices while YBM is pregnant will decrease her chances of giving birth to a child who will suffer from physical and mental health issues for the rest of their life? Did you know staying fit could also make YBM a little LESS crazy as she's carrying your legacy?

As soon as we started "trying," I tossed the booze, adjusted my diet, and established a better fitness routine. Even after Shanon became pregnant, I maintained these changes for her, our baby, and my health. It was a lot easier for us both to stay healthy when we did these things together, all the while prepping my swimmers for baby #2.

Your Purpose

EVERYTHING you put into your body goes into your sperm, and EVERYTHING that goes in YBM's body goes into the baby (including her emotions).

If you want to set your family up for success:

- Put down the booze

- Put out the smokes

- Pick up a carrot

- Sweat a little bit every day

Do you *have to* do these things? No, absolutely not.

Are you setting yourself up for avoidable complications during and after pregnancy if you don't? Yes, yes you are.

The value comes when you and YBM stay healthy **together**.

LEARN TO BREATHE

We faced several stress-inducing situations during Shanon's pregnancy, from layoffs to mudslides, and ER visits (hers and mine), to mental breakdowns (hers... ok, mine too). We had no choice but to get good at managing stress together. As a Marine Corps pilot, I often applied a version of the 4 X 4 breathing technique to counter the flood of adrenaline that came during high-stress situations. As an expecting Dad, I applied this in moments when emotions started to flare up, and it always helped bring us out of "seeing red" and into a state of mental clarity so we could calmly work through challenges together.

Your Purpose

Learn how to manage stress together *before* your baby comes (ideally before you're pregnant) so when that beautiful birth plan goes out the window, you know how to work through difficult situations with each other.

Here are a few ideas that brought about positive opportunities for us to practice stress management that you can try:

- Take road trips over 3 hours

- Survive a natural disaster

- Start a business

- Travel internationally with your in-laws

If you survive that last one, pregnancy will be a breeze!

<u>4 X 4 Breathing Technique</u>

1. Face your partner

2. Take them by both hands

3. Tell them to close their eyes

4. Breath in for a count of 1-2-3-4

5. Hold your breath for a count of 1-2-3-4

6. Breath out for a count of 1-2-3-4

7. Keep lungs empty for a count of 1-2-3-4

8. Repeat until they no longer want to inflict bodily harm on loved ones

(start with 4 cycles)

BE THE KEEPER OF THE DUE DATE

L ike most people, we told people the date our baby was "supposed" to be born. I honestly wish we had not, mostly because as the date approached, everyone wanted updates. *All. The. Time.* What started as a way to keep track of Shanon's progress, turned into the constant stressor of having to tell people "No, the baby has not come yet."

Shanon's 2 Cents: *It's stressful and annoying having friends and family constantly barrage you asking whether or not you've given birth yet. Getting not-so-subtle "check-ins" from well-wishers made me want to throw my phone out a window, book a one-way ticket to Timbuktu, and hide away in the jungle until I'd had time to figure out how to be a mom. When 40 weeks rolled around, the last thing I needed*

*was the world reminding me that—no shit—I hadn't had
a baby yet.*

Your Purpose

Lie, Lie, Lie!

Ok, you don't have to lie about your due date. But
remember, the only people who *need* to know when your
baby is due are your birth team, YBM, and you. The
estimated window for a typical delivery is anywhere from
37 to 42 weeks. Baby will come when baby is ready, so
rather than sharing the due date, share the month, or a
wide date range, and call it good.

SHOW UP FULLY

When we went to events, whether it was classes, meetups, yoga, or whatever, there was always at least one mom sitting alone or one couple where the partner was completely tuned out, (aka useless) and the expecting mom was hurting so bad for them to participate.

About the third time I saw this, I realized:

- It was NOT about the class

- It was NOT about yoga

- It was NOT about the event

It WAS about fully showing up with Shanon.

Shanon's 2 Cents: *When Matthew accompanied me to prenatal activities, we would get double the benefit. If I* *spent an hour getting a massage, he discovered new books to read and made friends with other expecting parents in the waiting room. If I zoned out in class, he took notes and asked a million questions. Not to mention, having an engaged and actively supportive partner show up with me as I'm waddling around is like bringing the hottest date to a party—it's a great ego boost.*

Your Purpose

It doesn't matter if the event is a:

- Birth class

- Maternity store grand opening

- Meet the doula mixer

What does matter is that you show up **with** her, and show up **fully**.

INVEST IN YOUR EDUCATION

I like sitting in classes listening to lectures as much today as I enjoy talking to customer service for hours on end. Although Shanon and I were only "required" to attend one prenatal class, we attended at least 5 different classes throughout her pregnancy. Sitting through 20+ hours of classes was not my favorite weekend activity, but it proved to be necessary to find out how much I did <u>not</u> know about her pregnancy. Granted, I played "Stump the Teacher" to make it more fun, and help me develop an informed opinion so I could help Shanon make critical decisions about our birth plans. Self-study is vital, but it has to be paired with guided education.

Shanon's 2 Cents: *For me, spending money on classes incentivizes me to attend them. Since I never dreamed of*

motherhood, I never played with dolls, and I never babysat, I
knew that unless I invested in birth prep classes, I wouldn't be
prepared for pregnancy or parenthood. Truthfully, I was in
so much physical discomfort during class that despite my best
efforts, I zoned out a LOT. Having Matthew there beside me
made me confident that our investment was worth the time
and money we spent learning about pregnancy, birth, and
beyond.

<u>Your Purpose</u>

When you attend classes, be where your feet are:

- Be present

- Put your phone away

- Ask lots of questions

It's the bare minimum you can do to positively contribute to your partner's pregnancy. You will no doubt have to practically apply what you learned in prenatal classes before your baby is born.

DEVELOP AN INFORMED OPINION

I realized *real* quick that if I wanted to have a say in Shanon's pregnancy, I had better get *real* smart *real* fast. No one could learn the ins and outs of what she was going through for me. There was no answer bank in the back of the textbook.

So, I read (ask me for my list of what NOT to read), watched documentaries (be ready for the uncensored version if you go this route), listened to podcasts (be careful with these rabbit holes of social media "experts"), interviewed medical providers (it is nerve-racking how different professionals in the same field have such varying opinions), and got a lot of weird looks when I asked more seasoned parents about their pregnancy experiences (it is still a taboo topic in the U.S.).

<u>Your Purpose</u>

Make yourself useful during this 40+ week marathon by becoming educated BEFORE your baby arrives. Think of this as getting ahead before you take the test. Read the books, do the research, and interview the professionals. This way, when, not if, YBM has a concern pop up, you will be better prepared to answer the question "Is this normal?" BEFORE she gets sucked into Reddit or WebMD.

Partner Pro-tip:

It is NOT about knowing everything.

It IS about knowing how to access the information you need to help make the best choices for YOUR growing family.

MAKE TIME FOR JUST THE TWO OF YOU

When we found out that Shanon was pregnant, we set out on a journey to see as much of the world as we could. We sold all of our worldly possessions, got in my truck, and drove without a deadline. After we completed a 10,000-mile road trip around North America, we proceeded to book a one-way ticket to Denmark and travel around Europe until Shanon could no longer fly comfortably.

As a final "just us" anniversary trip, we retreated to a cabin in the back woods of Indiana so Shanon and I could spend time together without outside distractions (we left our laptops at home and kept our phones in a kitchen drawer).

Looking back, now that we're a few months into operating as a family of 3, enjoying time as "just the two of us" was one of the best decisions we ever made.

Your Purpose

Life after having a baby WILL be different. Before baby enters your world:

- Travel together (or take a staycation).

- Spend time connecting and reconnecting in a way that is meaningful to you.

- Make the time to be alone with each other BEFORE your baby makes their appearance.

Enjoy the solitude and your relationship as you know it before you're operating on your tiny human's timeline and adjusting to a new dynamic.

BUILD YOUR BIRTH TEAM TOGETHER

S hanon and I interacted with over 25 different birth professionals throughout her pregnancy. Of the 25, 3 were at our birth—a midwife, an assistant midwife, and our doula. If we had any other group of people managing her birth, we would've probably been forced to transfer to a hospital. Because we put in countless hours interviewing, choosing, and getting to know our birth team TOGETHER, I was able to advocate for Shanon throughout her pregnancy and during labor. Additionally, having our doula at *my* side and on the same page ensured the medical team was able to manage the birth of our daughter safely and per our wishes.

Shanon's 2 Cents: *Pregnancy brain is real. Since it was hard for me to form fully coherent sentences, Matthew* *became my rock for communicating with our birth team. There were a couple of times when I wanted to rip people's heads off. Thankfully, he was able to manage the conversations and help us preserve our relationships with the people we entrusted with our birth.*

Your Purpose

Take an active role in choosing your doula, midwife, OB, witch doctor (or whoever you want on your birth team).

Your **medical team** (OB/midwife) is there to ensure YBM and your baby have a SAFE birth.

Your **doula** is your "big sister"—she's there to help you make hard decisions and advocate your wishes to your medical team (especially if things don't go as planned). She's also there to coach YOU so you can effectively support YBM during the actual birth.

Since both of you will interact with your birth team at different stages of the pregnancy, you **both** need to build those relationships. Period.

Make your birth plan(s) together

...AND REVIEW THEM BEFORE SHE'S IN LABOR

S hanon and I spent an entire day outlining our wishes in every possible situation from "if everything goes perfectly at home" to "emergency c-section." We did not want to have to workshop through difficult decisions as Shanon was laboring with the baby's head about to pop out. It was a tedious process, but it allowed us to be on the same page and convey our intent to our birth team early.

However, even with all of our prep work, we made our plans so far in advance that I missed a key element (Shanon did not want to push on her back unless medically necessary) while she was in labor. I didn't even realize the weight this bore until she told me about it weeks after our baby was born.

<u>Your Purpose</u>

Write your birth plan together and early and ensure everyone (medical team, doula, you, YBM, and anyone else attending your birth) has access to the document. No more Netflix & chill until the birth plan is done.

Writing your birth plan **together** will:

- Identify differences in beliefs and values you and YBM may have.

- Force you to talk through your options from cervical sweeps and drinking Glucola to "mandatory" shots and circumcision.

- Allow you to make difficult decisions together ahead of time.

- Ensure you, YBM, and your birth team are on the same page <u>before</u> your baby comes.

Partner Pro-tip: *Making a birth plan is like putting emergency road flares in your car trunk, they are useless if you don't know how to use them properly.*

Once you have your plan(s) in place:

- *Review them after every check-up (in case your medical situation changes)*

- *Communicate key elements to your medical providers (allergies, pushing positions, choices on baby care e.g. vitamin K and cord clamping, etc.)*

- *Have an updated print-out on hand*

Be prepared to help her manage changes, and advocate for her[1] to the medical team during labor.

---

1. If you don't feel prepared to take on this task alone or are a first-time parent, seek doula support.

RUB HER BELLY

Long before Shanon started to show, the last thing I would do before we went to sleep was rub her belly with anti-stretch mark lotion. What started as a technique to manage potential stretch marks turned into our nightly ritual and an exercise in intimacy. Over time, I completely forgot that this had anything to do with stretch marks. This became my way of making sure she felt a little pampered and taken care of each night before we closed out our day... and of course, I got to touch her boobs (with her consent).

Your Purpose

YBM will gain weight, her physical stamina will decrease, and she might get stretch marks. Honestly, you probably won't recognize her body by the end of her pregnancy.

Listen closely as you lotion her up:

It is NOT about putting on the lotion.

It IS about conveying to her that you appreciate her sacrifices for your family.

And oh, by the way, you get to touch her naked[1] ...

...need I say more?

---

1. Only with her consent

TALK TO YOUR BABY

BEST KICK IN THE FACE YOU WILL EVER GET

I loved this. Before she could even hear me, I told Baby Poppyseed about our plans, adventures, and how excited we were to meet her. Then, at about 30 weeks, she started talking back! I would say something and get a little *bump* or *boop* from Shanon's belly. By about week 36, her tummy would come to life when we had our daddy-daughter chats. No time spent in the Marines, no months of training or deployments, and no hardening of my emotions could have prepared me for what I felt when I realized my unborn baby had learned the sound of my voice.

Shanon's 2 Cents: *Watching Matthew talk to Baby Poppyseed let me get a sneak peek into what he would be like as a dad, which was as much of an oxytocin rush as goat yoga.*

It was adorable to see how much he loved her, even before she was born.

Your Purpose

Y'all, a soft moment here. Your baby is as alive inside that tummy as they will be when you hug them goodbye on their first day of school. They hear every word you say, so make sure you say something worthwhile.

As early as you can, get up close to YBM's belly and just start talking! Before you know it, that little alien inside will start to wiggle at the sound of your voice. It's truly a beautiful moment—for all of you.

READ OUT LOUD BEFORE BED

When we found out Shanon was pregnant, I set a goal to read to Baby Poppyseed every night for 30 days. The next thing we knew, 30 days turned into 41 weeks. We also found that taking the time to read every night helped us both wind down and sleep more soundly. Shanon and I both suffered from sleep issues long before our baby came along, and Shanon's insomnia worsened with pregnancy, so this unexpected benefit was a welcome surprise.

I found that when we shut off the technology and snuggled up for nightly "read-y time," I'd usually make it about half a chapter before I had a snoring mommy-to-be next to me, which would calm me to sleep shortly after.

<u>Your Purpose</u>

Read at least one book you're interested in *out loud* to your baby before they're born. Reading is the best way for you to deliberately teach your baby the sound of your voice while simultaneously helping YBM clean up her sleep hygiene and fight off pregnancy insomnia.

Partner Pro-tip: *If you're not able to read to YBM in person, send her a voice or video recording that can be played before she goes to sleep.*

HOLD HER HAND

When Shanon almost ate it on some black ice during our first winter walk in Chicago, I realized that holding her hand took on a whole new purpose. By holding her hand when we were out and about, I could tell when Baby Poppyseed was making her uncomfortable because Shanon would slow down. If she squeezed my hand in a social setting, I was alerted to the fact that something wasn't right, and would either find her a seat or get her out of the situation. If she forgot to laugh at one of my corny dad jokes, through no fault of her own of course, I would simply squeeze her to let her know that I was there for her, no matter what.

<u>Your Purpose</u>

No Cobra pilot ever operates without a co-pilot. You are the co-pilot now. No matter how independent YBM is, she NEEDS you to "cover her 6"—physically, like holding her hand on the ice, and emotionally, like getting her out of uncomfortable social situations.

The intent isn't to be overbearing or to stifle her independence, but to have her back.

Being the purposeful partner frees her mind to focus on nurturing, loving, and caring for your baby because she knows you are nurturing, loving, and caring for her.

SHOW HER YOU CARE

DON'T JUST TELL HER

During Shanon's pregnancy, I witnessed the mental rollercoaster she went through to acknowledge and accept her changing body. I saw her cry in the closet when she could no longer squeeze herself into her favorite shirt. I observed her becoming more reserved than usual when she had to modify her movements in yoga classes to accommodate her growing belly. Although I thought she was beautiful and wanted desperately for her to think the same, I learned that this was not a battle I could fight for her.

However, I COULD continue to show her that I loved her and found her sexy as hell by kissing her. Kissing her in public was my way of showing her that no matter what changes she went through, I would still choose her every time. She was (and is) my hottie with a naughty mommy body, and I won't let her forget it.

<u>Your Purpose</u>

SHOW her you care. If you're a physical person, hold her often, and hold her tight. If you're not, leave her notes around the house. Even a simple "I love you" on a sticky note will do.

YBM might be frustrated, irritable, and probably resistant at first.

You might compliment her, and receive a glare in return.

You might plan a date night and find her crying in the closet 5 minutes before you're supposed to leave.

DO NOT STOP TRYING.

Do not take her jabs personally and do not ever take your frustration out on her.

GRAB A FOOT AND START RUBBING

"Everything hurts and I'm dying..."

Ok, so maybe Shanon didn't say it exactly like that, but right around 20 weeks was when her soreness kicked in. It started in her lower back and spread to her hips, thighs, feet, and shoulders. Even with professional chiropractors giving relief in her last few weeks, the discomfort of carrying a watermelon and two cantaloupes around all day, every day, took a noticeable toll on her. I paid that toll with massages. Some may see this as extra work, but I saw it as yet another opportunity to be physically affectionate towards my (mostly) naked wife.

Your Purpose

You can learn how to give a safe prenatal massage, or just grab a foot and start rubbing. As pregnancy progresses, you can bet that her hips, back, and feet will be sore... all the time. This is less about being a pro and more about doing what you can to ease her physical discomfort.

If you can't be there in person to massage her yourself, help her book a prenatal massage, or send her a gift card so she can go get one...

...just make sure she's not getting a free rub down from the milkman.

CLIP HER TOENAILS

Shanon has always been very particular about her self-care routines. She has always been extremely independent when it came to things like facials, massages, and nail care, so I was surprised when she asked me to clip her toenails for her.

Similar to needing to help out with Shanon's pedicures, shaving anything below her waistline became a challenge once she could no longer see past her belly button. Since she wasn't big on other hair removal methods, yet didn't want to go full sasquatch, I also had to make sure my hand was surgeon steady with a razor.

<u>Your Purpose</u>

Help her out with self-care such as:

- Exfoliating

- Shaving

- Clipping toenails

- Putting shoes on

- Finding clothes that fit and are comfortable

All those little things make a HUGE difference in how she sees herself.

Partner Pro-tip: *When it's time for a bath or shower, be close by for "safety reasons" (or heck, just hop in there with her and scrub her back. wink wink).*

NAP WITH HER

I love naps. Never met one I didn't get along with. After over a decade in the Marines, I learned how to sleep almost anywhere—even a 15-minute power-up on the way to the store. I was usually a passenger for these. Once Shanon started growing our baby, her body told her to nap more, a lot more. This became a great excuse for us to nap together. Plus, skin-to-skin isn't only good for babies... if you know what I mean.

Shanon's 2 Cents: *The further along I got into my pregnancy, the more irrationally anxious I became. There were days when I would wake up from a nap crying because I had a nightmare that Matthew would go out for groceries and get run over by a car. I'm a fiercely independent person, but it's like a switch flipped, and I wanted to be around him ALL THE TIME. It was the worst feeling to go to sleep with* *him next to me and wake up not knowing where he went, even if it was just to the kitchen for midnight tacos.*

<u>Your Purpose</u>

During pregnancy, sleep is as precious as lithium-ion batteries in a Tesla factory. Just like a professional athlete or someone recovering from surgery, YBM's body is going to do its most efficient work when she is sleeping. 10, 12, or 14 hours of sleep a day is ok.

If she wants you around, try your best to be nearby, even when she's sleeping.

If she needs her space, don't take it personally, just let her rest in peace.

Partner Pro-tip: *If you can't be there in person, give her one of your hoodies to sleep in so she has that familiar comfort.*

Partner Pro-tip +1: *Keep something for yourself. YBM may want to be around you more and you should accommodate as much as possible. However, keep something as your "me time."*

MAKE HER A SANDWICH

IT'S ONE LESS THING ON HER PLATE

You know the saying "the woman's place is in the kitchen"? Yeah no. Not in this house. Cooking is about as stress relieving for Shanon as starting taxes on April 15th. So, once we found out Baby Poppyseed was on the way, meal prep was the first thing I "took off her plate." I watched a few YouTube videos, grabbed a mommy-to-be cookbook, and even recruited the family to help me stock the fridge.

When my sister visited us toward the end of Shanon's pregnancy, I spent 2 full days prepping soups and stews with her to prepare for the postpartum period. While my sister and I meal-prepped, Shanon got to decompress and laugh at our kitchen shenanigans. It was a great way to spend quality time together without overwhelming anyone.

<u>Your Purpose</u>

There is inevitably *something* YBM hates doing but does it anyway for the sake of the family such as:

- cooking

- washing and folding laundry

- taxes

- picking up dog poo

Whatever it is (and I KNOW you know what it is)—take it off her plate.

CONTINUE HONING YOUR BABY MAKING SKILLS

DON'T STOP BEING INTIMATE

Watching Shanon's body change, and seeing her maternal instincts start to kick in drove me wild. Even though we already had a very healthy sex life before Baby Poppyseed was conceived, once I found out that Shanon was pregnant, it was like a switch flipped and she became even MORE attractive. My favorite piece of advice from our birth team was to continue having sex as long as Shanon was still comfortable.

Shanon's 2 Cents: *Watching my body grow and morph was hard. Once I had to size up on stretchy pants, I stopped putting an effort into my appearance—it just seemed like a* *battle I couldn't win. I have never felt less sexy in my life. I'm grateful that Matthew never stopped trying to keep the spark alive, especially on days when I wanted to smash every mirror in the house.*

<u>Your Purpose</u>

Unless otherwise told by your birth team to stop having sex, DON'T! You are not going to dent the baby's forehead.

If one or both of you are just not feeling it in terms of having sex, that is ok. Hormones and libidos are going to fluctuate. Instead, you can still give massages, brush hair, hold hands, or cuddle up and watch cartoons.

Partner Pro-tip:

It is NOT about sex.

It IS about intimacy.

Do not let your intimacy shrink as her baby bump grows.

FIGHT OFF FOMO TOGETHER

(FOMO: FEAR OF MISSING OUT)

Shanon and I are extremely adventurous. Pre-pregnancy, our hobbies included dancing, hiking through pathless mountains, international shooting competitions, and skydiving. However, with Baby Poppyseed on the way, we had to pause and assess risk differently. There were a lot more consequences if either one of us got hurt.

That lesson sank in for me when we wanted to explore the Elie Chainwalk in Scotland. When we got to the trail, we realized it was more of a scramble on the cliffs than a relaxing walk on the beach. Additionally, the rocks were so slick from ocean spray that even though we had traveled across the Scottish peninsula to explore the beaches, we called it off.

Since then, whenever my skin tingled, or the hair stood up on the back of my neck, I learned not to push it. The time to take more risks would come again.

Shanon's 2 Cents: *It is terrifying to be responsible for growing a tiny human in your body. Trying to balance my unborn daughter's health and well-being with my need to explore, learn, and adventure was a challenge in and of itself. When Matthew proactively erred on the side of caution, it made me feel more supported and less like the party pooper.*

Your Purpose

Make sure YBM can enjoy life without feeling pressured to push herself beyond appropriate limits or to accept unnecessary risks. The time to be wild will come again.

In the meantime:

- Try new restaurants

- Build pillow forts

- Go to a comedy show

- Explore small towns near you

Do not let laying low be boring!

The value comes when you and YBM fight off FOMO **together**.

Partner Pro-tip: *Keep in mind that having options with plenty of seating and restrooms will always be a good starting point.*

MAKE SURE SHE ALWAYS HAS A PLACE TO SIT

...AND PEE

During our first anniversary getaway, we stopped at a leather shop to get me a new belt. In the middle of shopping, I noticed Shanon sitting on the floor in a corner. After checking in to make sure she was OK, I realized that she just needed a place to sit. Frankly, if I were carrying two grapefruits and a honeydew melon all day, I'd probably need to sit as well. From then on, if we were going to go out, go for a walk, go exploring, or anything that involved being on our feet for more than about 15 minutes, having a place to stop and "take a sitter" had to be part of the plan.

<u>Your Purpose</u>

Be on the lookout for places YBM can sit, and always know where the closest bathroom is. Kindly ask the able-bodied 17-year-old taking selfies in the handicapped seat on the subway to let YBM sit down. Check in with her often to make sure she isn't silently withering away in pain. If you don't, you may find her sitting on the ground, which is fine for a spring picnic, but not so much in the middle of a Chicago train station.

Plan accordingly. Pause as necessary. Pee frequently.

GIVE HER A LIFT

LITERALLY.

I didn't understand how the extra weight was physically affecting Shanon until her last trimester. When her back started hurting more frequently, I realized that the strain was a direct result of where our baby rested in her belly. That 7-pound baby came with about 35 additional pounds of placenta, blood, and other "baby goo." All that was constantly pulling against Shanon's lower back and pressing against her hips. Not knowing how to help, I went up behind her and lifted her belly in a half-thought-out attempt to ease her discomfort. Surprising as it was, the 'little lift' removed that pressure—and according to Shanon, it was fantastic.

<u>Your Purpose</u>

A helping hand goes a long way, 2 supportive ones go about 3 inches. The bump lift is just one example of a safe way to give YBM some physical relief from the constant pressure of carrying your baby.

Partner Pro-tip: *Take a prenatal "comfort measures" class to learn exactly what kind of massage and pressure work techniques will help manage YBM's physical discomfort.*

INVEST IN PILLOWS

Getting comfortable was hard for Shanon, so we tried all the pregnancy pillows. Just in case your brain misread that and you think we tried *a lot* of pillows, what I wrote was *All. The. Pillows.* Although there was not one "miracle" pillow that gave her constant relief, the "clamshell" pillow + a longer pillow between her knees seemed to help the most—especially towards the end of her 3rd trimester. Plus, this was the only pillow that allowed me to snuggle up to her at night.

However, even after all that, Shanon would get comfortable nestling herself in the best pillow configuration, just to have to get up to pee.

<u>Your Purpose</u>

Help YBM explore different pregnancy pillow options, but don't purchase any that don't come with free returns. It will take a while to find the "perfect" pillow configuration, but having that additional support will help ease some of the discomfort that comes with trying to sleep on her side while carrying a watermelon in her belly.

CUT THROUGH THE FOG

...THE BRAIN FOG

Shanon is smart. No, I mean borderline creative genius smart. So when pregnancy brain kicked in and she started forgetting things, mismatching her sentences, and cognitively operating in a fog, I would write down all of our questions and barrage the medical team at our weekly checkups. Whenever Shanon felt like something was "off," I texted and called our birth team until we had a full understanding of the situation. I had to become comfortable asking very specific questions and not stopping until I fully understood Shanon's situation. Even when we had to make an unexpected ER trip, I ran interference with the doctors and nurses to make sure we were all on the same page.

Shanon's 2 Cents: *I prefer trying to figure things out myself before asking for help, which usually means consulting "Dr. Google" before calling the midwife. Rational? Probably not. But it felt better than having the midwife reassure me (again) that I was experiencing a normal part of growing a human.*

Your Purpose

When in doubt, YOU figure it out:

- Take note of YBM's questions and concerns so you're aware of what and how she's feeling

- Pick up the phone and call the birth team

- Humble yourself and ask lots of questions during YBM's appointments

You are paying for their service, therefore you have the right to ask your providers every question you've ever had about pregnancy. Do not force YBM to find the answers on her own.

FILTER YOUR FEED

PRESERVE YOUR MENTAL HEALTH

I stopped ingesting any baby-related social media at about month 6 of Shanon's pregnancy because it was just garbage. When Shanon came to me with something negative she read online, it just added to both of our stress. Knowing that I could not tell her to stop, I stopped instead. Honestly, I did not miss it after about a week. More importantly, it gave me the ability to help her manage her anxiety from ingesting the inevitable negativity she read when she was on various apps and forums.

<u>Your Purpose</u>

Brace yourself. People will want to share every detail you *never* asked for about their pregnancies, *especially if it didn't go as planned*. Since there's only so much you can do to re-direct or avoid those conversations, you can instead:

- Find her positive birth stories

- Connect with people who had good experiences

- Manage your media intake and screen unnecessary and anxiety-inducing information

And for the love of gorgonzola, find a tactful way to tell the negative & nosy Nancies in your life to kindly...

...fuck off.

BUILD YOUR NEST TOGETHER

I didn't care what blankets we had during our 10,000-mile road trip in the back of my truck as long as we didn't freeze to death. I didn't care what hotels we stayed in during our 15-country journey around Europe as long as we had a bed to sleep in. When it came to furnishing our apartment in Chicago, I didn't care where we hung the pictures or what color the throw pillows were.

But Shanon did.

These things were important to Shanon and made a difference to her. I learned that saying "I don't care" actually translates to "This is not important to me," which was not fair to her. After all, she was putting in the time, effort, and energy to make this space our home. The least I could do was give her my feedback when she asked for it.

Your Purpose

You're probably going to spend a LOT of time at home once your baby comes, so take the time to make your space comfortable. From picking pillow colors and assembling new baby furniture to arranging and rearranging the layout of that furniture, helping YBM make the little decisions will have a very positive impact on your partnership.

Remember, she asks you to participate because she values your opinion.

Partner Pro-tip: *You do not have to do things the traditional way. If you want to build out a whole nursery and get every bell and whistle there is, go for it! If you want to convert your living room into a giant foam-floor playpen lined with pillows, and mattresses with a stripper pole as the centerpiece, we can give some design recommendations.*

The value comes when you and YBM build your nest ***together***.

SKIP THE FLOWERS AND CHOCOLATE

RUN TO GET HER SLIP-ON SHOES

O f all the pregnancy "must haves," the hands-free or slip-on shoes were what Shanon raved about the most. Before getting a pair, I had to use pliers to pull her boots on at one point. Needless to say, the slip-ons were a vast improvement both in utility and comfort.

Shanon's 2 Cents: *I tried on a Kardashian's closet worth of shoes before caving into targeted Instagram ads and buying a pair of slip-on sneakers. Bending over to tie my shoes became an Olympic sport when I could no longer see past my belly button. These shoes and pregnancy pillows made life as a mama manatee 10,000 times easier.*

<u>Your Purpose</u>

Put down this book.

Go get her slip-on shoes.

That is all.

TAKE BUMPIES

The documentation didn't need to be anything formal or fancy, but I knew having a growing bump photo album at the end of Shanon's pregnancy would be invaluable to look back on. We took a "Poppyseed Bump picture" in the same pose every chance we got. I can't wait to embarrass Baby Poppyseed in front of all her friends when I pull out this album!

"bumpin" 28 WKS

16 WKS

"we're ready" 40 WKS

"we did it!" 4 WKS

"Get out!" 41 WKS

"patience" 36 WKS

<u>Your Purpose</u>

There is no doubt that YBM will be self-conscious about being in pictures as she grows, but finding a fun way to document the pregnancy journey will pay dividends after it ends. Find some cool backgrounds, set up some special occasions, and have fun preserving your memories together. Plus, it's a great opportunity to give mommy's tummy a raspberry right before the shutter clicks.

ENFORCE HER BOUNDARIES

Shanon wanted as few people in the room as possible for her birth. Being surrounded by people stresses her out—especially if it's medical staff. I knew that this was one of the moments where regardless of what anyone else wanted, my role was to enforce her boundaries and cover her 6. It was our birth experience, but ultimately, Shanon's choice.

Truthfully, if we had had it our way, it would have just been me, her, our baby, and the Uber driver. Maybe next time...

Shanon's 2 Cents: *Treat this as an exercise of consent. In sex, if one partner consents and the other does not, the ultimate "right to decide" goes to the non-consenting partner. It becomes sexual assault if you pressure someone into doing something they don't want to do with their body. Childbirth is no different. It's my body, so I get to set the boundaries.*

If you need me to spell it out even more:

I'm the one pushing out a baby.

I'm the one who is bloody, naked, in pain, and at my most vulnerable.

I get the final say.

<u>Your Purpose</u>

What she said.

BE FLEXIBLE

We got a lot better at giving ourselves grace when changing or canceling plans. As much as we enjoyed going out and being social, Shanon's body seemed to have an automatic off switch around 9:00 pm. Although we still traveled, went out to dinners & networking events, and attended balls & weddings, I knew not to plan for anything too late, or I might find her asleep in a corner. Rather than seeing this in a negative light, I reminded myself that the more rest mommy got, the better Baby Poppyseed would grow. We learned to rally when Shanon had the energy and gave ourselves the grace to go home early when she didn't.

Shanon's 2 Cents: *It was a blow to my self-confidence when my weight and shape prevented me from being as active as I was before I got pregnant. I was so afraid of being a* party pooper, that at first, I tried to push myself to stay out late—even when I felt my body shutting down. I didn't want to be the reason Matthew and I became "boring." Although we had to adjust our lifestyle around my needs, Matthew never made me feel bad for being pregnant. He was patient, and attentive, and never let it show if he was disappointed that I couldn't rally.

<u>Your Purpose</u>

Make your plans and get excited about the adventures while being prepared to flex in the moment. Never think twice about skipping something to preserve the health and wellness of your baby, YBM, or yourself.

For big events like weddings you cannot physically attend, FaceTime. For professional events that you cannot make in person, Zoom. For those times when YBM just wants to stay home:

- Snag the foot lotion

- Make some popcorn

- Snuggle up for a Hallmark movie-marathon date night in bed

You will NEVER regret making those memories.

LET HER CRY

One Saturday afternoon towards the end of Shanon's pregnancy, we were in bed weathering the Chicago winter when Shanon reached over to grab her iPad off the nightstand. As she did, it slipped out of her hand and landed square on her face. Even though it didn't seem like a hard hit, it caused a very big cry to come—big hard tears that kept on for a while. After a few minutes, I realized that the crying was not about her ouchy on the outside at all.

Your Purpose

Just let her cry. I know you will want to understand what caused it, diagnose it, and fix it, but now is not the time. When she cries, *and she will*, just:

- Hold her close

- Tell her she is safe

- Let the wave of whatever emotion is *really* happening come and go

Once the wave has passed, and she is ready (though she might never be, that is ok), listen calmly, hold her, and just **BE THERE**.

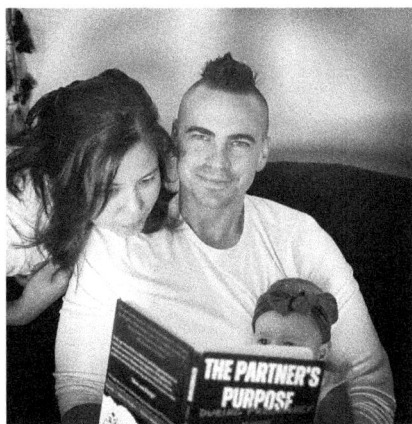

<u>Meet Matthew</u>

With the boldness of a Texan, the daring of a former Marine Corps Cobra pilot, and a touch of whimsy embodied in his trademark mohawk, **Matthew Morris** captivates audiences worldwide as an author and public speaker. His debut book, "The Partner's Purpose During Pregnancy," emerged from a 41-week journey across 15 countries, driven by his desire to support his wife, Shanon, during her pregnancy. Now fully immersed in the joys and complexities of new fatherhood, Matthew continues his writing journey while eagerly plotting future adventures with his growing family. Simultaneously, he remains dedicated to his role as a dynamic public speaker, inspiring and guiding communities worldwide in building and nurturing resilient relationships.

Looking for more?

Connect with us

www.thepartnerspurpose.com

IG @thepartnerspurpose